this modern love

will darbyshire

**For all those in love, out of love,
and everything in between**

Will Darbyshire is a 23-year-old British film-maker.
He has over one million followers across his YouTube,
Instagram and Twitter channels. His videos span
a range of subjects including relationship advice,
mental health issues, career plans, popular culture
and travel. This is his first book.

contents

Fragile.

Olivia
Pennsylvania, USA

this modern love

In the summer of 2014, I experienced a break-up. It was my first. And I was devastated.

Coping with the demise of my relationship was unlike anything else I'd ever felt before. Someone in my family told me that it was like coping with a death: you grieve in the same way; you're mourning the loss of a person. I suppose that's just how I felt: empty and lost, like a piece of me had broken off and crumbled, never to return.

Being an introvert and prone to bouts of anxiety, rather than telling all the people I knew and loved about my problems, instead I took to the strangers of the internet to express my thoughts and feelings. It was daunting at first, but gradually it started to make me feel better. It soon became soothing and cathartic, something I even enjoyed. Words would pour out of me in blog post after blog post and I began to make short films in an attempt to exhaust my emotions. I was still unhappy, but at least I was moving in the right direction. I was being productive.

→ Then something surprising happened, something I had never intended. People started responding, particularly to the YouTube videos I was making. The viewing figures grew and I realised my thoughts were being revealed to hundreds and then thousands of people. It was scary. Overnight I sort of became a faux 'agony aunt'. I would receive tens of emails every day from people suffering with heartbreak, who like me needed to offload their feelings. I felt myself personally connecting with people I had never met; all of us binding together to absorb, digest and move on from our experiences.

After a while, the tens of emails became hundreds and my own personal well of knowledge and emotion began to run dry. The cathartic hobby had blossomed into something bigger and much more important than me. I felt there needed to be a better forum for people to express themselves, and so the idea for *This Modern Love* was born.

This book, and the project as a whole, is an attempt to provide a safe environment for people to share their thoughts on modern relationships. Over the course of a year, I asked people from all over the world a series of questions and chronicled their responses in the collection of pages that you are about to read. The responses range from letters to pictures to single words, many from far-flung places, often in beautiful languages, always with searing honesty. They highlight the extremes and the humdrum of modern relationships, the large gestures and the tiny nuances that make people tick.

Love in the modern age is a complex idea. We're more connected then we've ever been, but with that comes its own set of problems. We're able to maintain relationships over larger distances but we sacrifice our primal need to be physical, to touch, to feel. What seemed impossible a decade ago is quickly becoming the norm, and online behaviour is revolutionising the way we think about love and how we interact with each other.

But does our online connection really make us closer? Does the distance allow us real happiness or heartbreak? I'd like to think the book answers some of these questions, but it also poses many more. Some of the letters are bitter, some of them are raw. Some of them are thankful, and some of them might make you laugh. But they have all made me think about some of our most fundamental needs and desires. And I hope they will do the same for you.

15,570
total responses

3,099
in our Gmail inbox

3,000
messages in our Tumblr inbox

58
'physical' letters by snail mail

7,924
words for 'love' on Instagram

1,489
tweets
#thismodernlove

the process

In order for *This Modern Love* to work, the project needed to be as easy as possible for people to participate in, whilst also having enough scope to appeal to a wide range of people with different experiences. So I devised a series of online posts. These posts would take the shape of a series of questions. And these questions were designed to provoke a response and get people thinking.

These were the six questions asked:

1. What would you say to your ex, without judgement?

2. Write a thank you note to your partner – describe or share (in a photo) the big and little things that make you happy.

3. What single word sums up your love life, your partner, or someone you like?

4. What single image sums up your love life, your partner, or someone you like?

5. What would you say to a crush? Write a letter to them to express it.

6. How has technology affected your relationship, either positively or negatively? Describe your experience.

11

Algeria	El Salvador	Israel	Mauritius	Puerto Rico
Angola	England	Italy	Mexico	Qatar
Argentina	Estonia	Jamaica	Morocco	Romania
Armenia	Finland	Japan	Nepal	Russia
Australia	France	Jordan	Netherlands	Saudi Arabia
Austria	Germany	Kazakhstan	New Zealand	Scotland
Bahrain	Greece	Kenya	Norway	Serbia
Belarus				Singapore
Belgium				Slovakia
Belize				Slovenia
Benin				South Africa
Bhutan				South Korea
Brazil		**98**		Spain
Brunei		**countries**		Sri Lanka
Bulgaria				Sweden
Canada		main demographic		Switzerland
Chile		16–24		Taiwan
China				Thailand
Colombia		youngest contributor		Trinidad and Tobago
Costa Rica		12		Turkey
Croatia				Ukraine
Curacao		oldest contributor		United Arab Emirates
Cyprus	Guam (USA)	81	Kuwait	Pakistan
Czech Republic	Honduras	Latvia	Panama	United States
Denmark	Hungary	Lebanon	Paraguay	Uruguay
Dominican Republic	Iceland	Lithuania	Peru	Venezuela
Ecuador	India	Luxembourg	Philippines	Vietnam
Egypt	Indonesia	Malaysia	Poland	Wales
	Ireland	Malta	Portugal	Zimbabwe

The six questions were spread out over six months. Each one was posted publicly on my social media pages. For the simpler (or at least, shorter) questions I would use only Twitter or Instagram and the hashtag #thismodernlove. For the more expansive questions, which required a letter, I would make a YouTube video to accompany each post, and then we set up email and Tumblr accounts for people to submit their responses to. We also managed some good old-fashioned postboxes in the UK and US (the number of digital letters was far greater than the physical, but I cherished every handwritten note). It took some experimenting to find the right social platform for the right question. In an attempt to reach an older demographic, I also reached out to a number of organisations that helped provide some context about relationships. (A big shout out to OnePlusOne for all their wonderful help, and for spreading the word on their forums, The Couple Connection and The Parent Connection. Their expertise was invaluable.)

I have to admit that gathering everything together was a gruelling and sometimes tedious process. There was just so much to go through: thousands upon thousands of emails, Tumblr messages, tweets, Instagram comments and piles of envelopes. It was a blessing and a curse, and after a while a colour-coded spreadsheet became my closest friend (something I thought I would never say). But whenever I was tired or overwhelmed by the project, whether late at night or early in the morning, without fail I would come across a letter that would floor me with a single expression, or a line that perfectly summed up a feeling that I had never been able to articulate before. That made it all worth it.

Eventually I was able to narrow the submissions down to a shortlist. Then with my lovely editor (hello, Ben) we printed

→ everything and sorted the sea of paper into two very large piles. It was incredibly difficult making the final selection; every letter was deeply personal and powerful in its own way. I agonised over every 'yes' and 'no'. But after hours, days and eventually weeks of deliberating, not to mention the occasional argument, we decided on a final list.

That final selection is this book, and the letters are structured into three parts. It felt natural doing it this way; after all, every love story has a beginning, a middle and an end. The first section focuses on the pre-relationship stage, the all-consuming 'crush' period that many of us will wince at with embarrassment when looking back, but at the time is everything. The second part focuses on partners in relationships: the personal strength that teamwork can provide; the challenges that collectively can be overcome; the nagging itch of commitment as passion fades. The final part examines, in unflinching detail, and in myriad ways, the break-up phase. Although modern love is impossible to ever completely contain or define, it seemed quite instinctive early on to frame the book with these headings.

I'm not going to say too much more. I have written short introductions to each section in the book, but as with the book as a whole, I've tried to let the letters speak for themselves, and not to pass on any of my own morals or judgements. For this reason, all of the letters included in the book have been printed as they were submitted – no edits or corrections of grammar or punctuation. I think they are raw and authentic this way, and in many cases the occasional idiosyncratic use of language reveals far more about the writer and the subject than if it had been 'corrected'.

Scattered throughout the book are some photographs that

I have taken, which I hope may reflect some of the themes or images in the letters. Any photograph that has a name underneath it was submitted as part of the project. You will also notice lists of words on some pages. No, these are not my attempts at avant-garde poetry, as lovely as these combinations are. These were actually the words submitted for the question, 'What single word sums up your love life, your partner, or someone you like?'

Whatever way you look at it, love is important. It might just be the single most important thing that we as humans can offer or receive. So, reader, I hope this book finds you in a good place; and, if it doesn't, I hope you find some solace reading about others' experiences. If the book is half as enjoyable and liberating for you as it was for me putting it together, it will have succeeded.

Finally, a massive thank you to every single person who contributed to *This Modern Love*: the talented writers, photographers and lovers. Thank you all for allowing me to read through your wonderful thoughts. At times I felt uncomfortable reading such personal stories; thank you for trusting me. Your letters are this book and you are the authors. I hope that seeing your words in print (or as an ebook) can provide you with a physical memory of your experiences, or a new perspective that you can take hold of. Even if your letter wasn't chosen, I can't thank you enough for sharing and making this what it is. It's an honour. Seriously.

Will
23, UK

This Modern

Kemp House

152 City Ro

~~London~~

EC1U 2NX

Royal Mail
South Midlands
Mail Centre
21-12-2015
64801869

Love

beginning

Waiting.

Alice
Glasgow, UK

beginning

Do you like me? Yes or no?

These are the questions you'll unfortunately have to ask someone at some point.

No matter what age you are, or what interests or background you have, these fundamentals decide everything. Do you like me? Would you like to be romantically involved with me? Are you sure?

Inevitably, with time and experience our personalities change. Due to the lives we lead we sometimes become less open to putting ourselves 'out there'; less willing to allow ourselves to be vulnerable. But that feeling of rejection or success rarely changes. It always transcends.

$\rightarrow$

confounding

tantalising

elusive

unattainable

tumultuous

unreachable

untimely

breathtaking

catastrophic

chaotic

forbidden

star-crossed

Nobody likes feeling heartbroken and I suppose that's why crushes are so damn terrifying. We walk around longing to have an interaction with our chosen special person, pining for any opportunity we can get to 'charm' them. In my case, that usually goes badly. I try my best, but the results are mixed, to be generous – I'm definitely below average on the charisma scale.

Once we've tried our luck at 'charming', it's up to the other person to decide whether or not we might suit them. We put ourselves through all of that just to find out a single answer, and I think that alone speaks volumes. If we as humans are willingly opening ourselves up for rejection, it must be for something important.

And a crush is important. It's the beginning of a relationship. It lays the foundations for everything to come. And despite being daunting, frankly terrifying territory, it's surprisingly a time we look back on fondly.

Although the practicalities of having an infatuation are scary, we often couldn't feel happier when we are in its grips. During this period we're in a drunken-like haze of stares and grins. We feel euphoric. People even tell us we look better. After all, how often do we feel like this?

In this book I explore the good as well as the not-so-good times in relationships.

Love is a mixed bag of emotions and the initial forays of any relationship illustrate this. The following letters show the extraordinary range of written testimonies that we received about love's first bloom. There were so many powerful and $\rightarrow$

moving submissions that sadly could not be included, but many of these chosen letters do represent similar sentiments that were shared by others.

The funny thing about reading the letters together was that they all evoked similar emotions. That giddy feeling when you first meet someone on your wavelength is persistent throughout your life and doesn't wear away over time. You could be 45 or 85 and still experience it like you did when you were 15. When reading these letters I felt myself transported to my younger self. Being in the throes of passion is something we've all been through and it's something we all remember.

Dearest love,

You're like a laughing piano.

You make me swim and drown, I can't bear your beautiful presence in my mind yet I never want you to leave, you are my Sunday best and my blue Monday.

You are my biggest contradiction and you make me see for miles.

All my love,

Aisling
Dublin

Dear ——,

It's strange to be writing you a letter because in my
head I'd go straight up to you and tell you exactly
how I feel, and you'd wear a smile the size of London
Bridge and tell me you feel exactly the same.

However, that's all in my head. When I see you
the only reason why you'll take a look is because
you're probably thinking why's his face so red?

That's what happens when I see you. You can call it
embarrassment, I call it annoying but I guess that's
my mind and heart saying I have grown feelings for
you and I'm happy I have. Really I am. I hope one day
you will too.

Speak to you soon (or just notice the effervescent
blush).

-S-R-

Dear **Josh**

Although we are good friends, I don't know how to tell you that I have had the biggest crush on you since the first day I saw you in my English class.

I mean, how do I tell you that I like you when I haven't even told anyone that I'm gay.

We talk so much and you probably think of it as a normal conversation but to me... It's more. It's an escape from the reality. The reality of a guy who lays in bed wishing that he was in an alternate universe, one in which both him and you would fall in love with each other.

I guess that's just wishful thinking. I can accept that we will only be friends but I just wanted you to know that you're beautiful and I love you.

Anonymous

Dear —— ,

You are like that one piece of artwork in an art gallery that people spend a little longer admiring.

Rosa
UK

Dear —,

I saw you the other day in the crowded dorm elevator.
Many people were pressed together but the only
person I noticed was you. I'd never seen you around
before and you immediately caught my eye. At
the sight of you, a daydream started to play in my
head as the elevator made its way to my stop on
the eighth floor.

Something about you made me yearn to get to know
you. I still do. Even though I knew it was a long shot,
I found myself disappointed when you didn't get off
on my floor.

I still replay the glances I stole of you in my head and
I kick myself for being so shy. I hope to run into you
again someday.

Alli
Montana, USA

Dear **Mr. Future Crush**,

Right now you are frustratingly just a figment of my
imagination, something I daydream about in times of
loneliness or boredom.

Before going to sleep I idly wonder what you're going
to be like, however that's like trying to imagine
a new colour.

So instead you take the form of a happy song,
the smell of a cologne, the hero in a novel.

You're a collage of all my happy moments and a sense
of comfort during the sad ones.

It's silly I know – even though we've never met I can't
help but feel a strange sense of longing and hope.

All I know is that whoever you are, you're going to be
amazing.

(Perhaps one day) yours,

Mivi
Wales

P.S. You better like pizza.

Dear ——,

When you'd run a sleepy hand through your tangled
hair, my heart would crumble to sugar. I would've
told you too, but every time I tried my throat closed
up all tight. I had to turn away.

Happy Valentine's Day
x

Sari

forelsket

a Norwegian word for the euphoria you experience
when you are first falling in love

Delilah
USA

Dear **crush**,

I remember the first time I got to Skype you.

The way I felt when we laid (what felt like next to
each other) in silence. Blissful silence that can only
be described as extraordinary. My heart jumped
and butterflies flew into my chest. My lips permanently
wore a smile. Even when you weren't looking at me or you
were distracted with other things, I still felt incredible.

I watched your facial expressions and examined your
features. Your beautiful face made me grin uncontrollably,
giggle like a child and blush scarlet red. When you told
me I was perfect I swear my heart literally skipped a beat.
I was unable to reply. Breath taken. Speechless.

Out of my sixteen years of living this is one of my fondest
memories. You made me feel loved and wanted, and for
once I didn't care about my appearance.

I only cared about you.

Love,

Isobel
England

Dear **Conner**,

I love a lot of things.

I love seeing old ladies' faces when you buy something off them in a charity shop, I love the smell of burnt out candles, I love Kendrick Lamar, and I love the short prickly noise between songs on a record.

I love a lot of things in this world, and I would love for another person to enjoy all these things with me.

Basically what I am saying is that I like you, so please come enjoy Kendrick Lamar with me, thanks.

Abbie
Scotland

D,

You amaze me.
You irk me.
You frustrate me.
You make me laugh.

I don't want to idolize you.
I am content with being your friend.
I'm proud of you,
who you have become and are becoming.

I'll be rooting for you.

M
Los Angeles, USA

Dear **Jack**,

Hello. I'm probably one of the only flutists that would admit they would date a brass player. Hell, I would scream it from the roof of the school if you shared the same feelings. Your actions and lack of words have made it very clear that you don't feel the same way as I.

I just wanted you to know that I don't care that you're very attractive, popular, and work out a lot (although it doesn't hurt). You're much more than that. I'm interested in the fact that you are extremely intelligent, funny, share my religion, and you have an amazing taste in classical music. You show an insane amount of care for your family, our school, and our community.

I just thought you should know that there are people out there that pay attention to your lovely character, and not just your 'cool' hair.

Hugs and smiles,

Jordan
Ohio, USA

Hi **Matt**

I like you but I don't want to ruin our friendship.

I'm the one that sent you the rose that you left in class.

Yasmin
Cheltenham

To **my crush**,

You're the reason for the soft smile upon my face,
the reason for my rosy cheeks and racing heart.

Thank you, just for being you.

Hannah
Connecticut, USA

Dear **Drake**,

When we both sat in a three hour lecture
and I instantly knew you were quoting Coldplay.

I called you out on it, your cheeks turned red, and we
threw our heads back laughing.

And in that moment, the crinkles by your eyes and the
curve of your smile,

I fell a little harder for you.

Your little one,

Em
(Emily)
USA

Dear **Jon**,

I know we have been married for almost 5 years but
I think it's important that I remind you that you are
still my crush. Still the boy I swoon over, who gives me
butterflies and makes me giggle.

I love everything about you, but I fell in love with your
heart first. Your giving spirit and your generosity.
Your ability to make people smile and laugh. Your
willingness to love and trust.

We have been through so much together; ups
and down, good and bad, and after it all you still
wake up every day with the desire to make me happy.
You have never been much of a talker, and that's
alright, because you don't show love with only your
words. You show love every time you make me laugh.
Every time you look across the room and catch my
eye. And every time you hold my hand and kiss my
forehead. I am beyond blessed to have you as my
crush, my husband, my best friend.

I just want to thank you for changing my life. Showing
me that even though two people have been together for
a long time the excitement doesn't have to diminish.
The love doesn't have to fade. Thank you for loving me,
needing me, and wanting me. Here is to 60 more years.
I love you.

Love,

Darlene
Ohio, USA

Dear **Crush**,

I'm Audrey, that girl you've known your whole life, that family friend's daughter that you've seen many times before, and the girl who you shared your many child secrets with.

I just wanted to say that I have a crush on you. Wow, that sounds so informal.

Yes, you are the crushee and I am the crusher, but do not be intimidated; do not be fooled; I am not in love with you.

You are that charismatic boy that has simultaneously won the genetic lottery and has managed to be experiencing a happy life, that boy that miraculously has happily married parents.

My whole life, I've admired you by the way you look and act; you live to make someone smile. You don't pass a day without happiness.

I remember the day when we were young and were best friends, before any feelings started infiltrating our hearts.

As the days passed though, and we grew, my feelings for you grew too.

I saw you change from this boy to a young man who still lives for a smile, grin or laugh. I saw the love that you give and need to become the great person of your future story. Your life. How am I not supposed to fall for that?

Today you live your days in a different environment from mine, a different country. You live your days and live your emotions without my knowledge; which I cannot bear.

For 6 years now we've been apart, we've grown that boundary that teenagers grow when they realize that they are too cool for anyone to be in their realm of existence.

For 6 years, I have been thinking about you; analyzing our interactions that are so precious, so rare. And I've been a coward.

For 6 years I've noticed that you noticed me too, you thought about me too, but I can't bring myself to do anything about it. I regret so many opportunities that I've passed up because when I see you, I freeze; my head freezes and my heart freezes. I hate that.

$\rightarrow$

47

I am a person, who embraces her awkwardness
and freckles. I am trying to find who I am, but how am
I supposed to do that when I'm thinking about you?

You have no idea how I feel about you, and you don't
think about me, but I know how I feel about you,
and I can ensure you that it isn't love.

I don't know what love is, I've never experienced it,
considering I am only 15.

I could say that I love you, but that would be a lie.
Because I can't love.

I can't love someone who is growing away from me.
I can't love someone who is oblivious of my feelings.
I can't love someone that I see twice a year; although
we live 10 minutes away from each other.

I can say that I love you if and when we will be
together. If I find courage and you find courage
and we are together, I will finally be able to say that
I am in love with you. When I can say that you are
mine, and that our frail hearts are both exposed to
a world of potential hurt, I will admit that you are my
first great love.

For now, I am substituting our potential love with a crush. I have a crush on you, and I can live with that.

I have found someone who I like, but don't love, to discover myself. Who knows? Maybe one day I will love him and I could say that he was my first great love.

Even when I say this, I know that you will be my first love.

So I will end with this; I have a crush on you, and if you want to do anything about that you know where to find me. I'll be waiting.

Tu sais qui tu es.

Love,

Audrey

Hey,

You probably don't realise this, but I quite like you.

You helped me fight my battles even though you were going through battles of your own.

You present yourself to the world as someone who doesn't care for much, but I can see you. You have a beautiful soul, that I would look after with all I have would you let me.

I'll always be here for your midnight calls and any other time you need me,

Amy
Switzerland

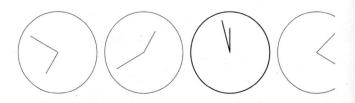

absent

unaware

longing

taciturn

timid

unobtainable

bittersweet

waiting

incipient

under construction

anticipation

lingering

sassy

tenacious

stuck

inseparable

taken

engaged

dear **aaron**,

i don't even know you but i think you're really cute. we've never spoken, but i'd rather like to at some point!

i'm not entirely sure if you've even noticed me, but i quite like seeing you sitting across the canteen every day.

we've made eye contact a few times! i don't know if that means anything though.

a couple days i plucked up the courage to add you on facebook, and you accepted! cheers for that!

the thing is though, i'll probably never end up getting to know you at all. so this is my letter to you, the confession you'll never read.

keep doing your hair the way you do!

lots of kinda-like,

jane

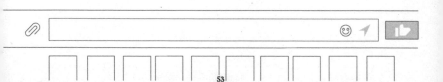

Dear **Oscar**,

I'm not sure of the kind of crush I have on you. I find you incredibly sexy, but I don't want to have sex with you. Your gait. Your beard. The intelligence behind your eyes. The private conversations we have on Messenger when we're at little parties together.

I don't want to be with you – in fact I can't be with you because of that girlfriend you've had for four years... but I want to spend time with you. You had me and my friends believing you wanted more with me – as French men do, but the coldness of your shoulder made me feel silly. You come from the cold and dark of poetry, and I come from the warmth and sun of life.

But you're someone I want to know. And I will, I'm determined to. I dream of having a coffee together in that corner of Paris where Hemingway and de Beauvoir frequented. I want to sip on coffee and have those conversations you and I long to have with each other – to be the modern day intellectuals we think we are.

You leave for Paris soon, and I hope to see you there.

H
American in France

Dear **Faded Nostalgia**,

We never made it, we tried but you decided it was time to stop kidding ourselves, were the one to speak the truth. Yet here I am once again listening to the music that is so distinctly you and thinking about all the things that painfully remind me that I could never actually hate you. Once again you've become the faded memory of the boy that I'll probably never meet again, that I'll never truly know and that's okay. I'll know who is calling if the number is blocked.

Sleepless Dreamer
Ireland

Dear **You**,

I done a lot of screaming
this weekend. Catching my
breath.

You find a way to do that
to me even if you're not
here.

I went out running trying
to shake that feeling.
Confused.

Why does the universe bring
people together and then tear them
apart?

Our lives don't collide really.
We come from different places.
Unusual.

We met out in nowhere,
I had this feeling someone
sent you.

Everything in this universe
has a chance to clash.
Everything.

From electrons to galaxies.
Anyway I'm glad I bumped
into you.

Cuz all those little bumps
we get helps us stay
intact.

Molly
Sweden

Dear **Crush**

I hardly know you. You're a friend of a friend.

We've only spoken a few times, normally about
me and my friend's weirdness, but in those brief
conversations I feel something strange and alien to
me. It feels like the butterfly catchers' butterflies
have escaped in my stomach, the fish's bubbles from
Finding Nemo just erupted from my chest and there
are ballerinas dancing on my heart. But every time
I fall into the pools of blue, which are in the middle of
your sclera, I start internally crying. For I know you
don't feel the same way, I know I am not on your mind
every living second and I know you hardly see me as
a friend. I'm a friend of a friend. You hardly know me.
But I am crushed by this crush.

In conclusion I have two things to say.

I really, really like you and damn you, hormones.

Bella
Wiltshire, UK

I know the question was, what *would* you say to your crush... but because I'm ballsy these have already been sent. Here are two letters that I wrote to crushes in 2015. The first letter I wrote to one of my good friends "jokingly" but not really... lol. The other one I wrote to someone who I was in a gap year program with. I knew that I would never see him again after the program ended, so I gave him a letter with a flower inside of it at the end... because I'm embarrassing as fuck. ughhhh...

C-Dawg,

This is hard for me to write
Because we're so damn tight
And this might sound conceited
But I'll say it anyway cuz our love be so undefeated

I rarely meet humans in this world
Who are just as smart and funny as your girl (<--me)
But you are an exception
Cuz at our friendship's conception
I realized you were poppin'
And that no matter what you did
You would always be at the top toppin'

You're awesome, my friend
Keep doing you, this ain't the end
You will always be someone I cherish, Farris. (<--you)
Saying goodbye is cruddy
But I will always be here for you...

Much love,

Your Netflix Buddy

Jon,

I'm not exaggerating when I say I've never had
a conversation like the one I had with you in my
room. I don't even know if you remember, but
I will be eternally grateful. You made me feel safe
and important, like my words and feelings mattered,
and you didn't push any unwanted advice on me but
still managed to try to understand and help. It was
extremely selfless and kind of you. Thank you. A
quote from the movie *Before Sunrise* (I know I keep
mentioning it, sorry, but watch it please) is:

> "I believe if there's any kind of God it wouldn't
> be in any of us, not you or me but just this
> little space in between. If there's any kind of
> magic in this world it must be in the attempt
> of understanding someone sharing something.
> I know, it's almost impossible to succeed but
> who cares really? The answer must be in
> the attempt."

I regret that I didn't make the effort to have more conversations with you like that, but I just didn't want to annoy you. I want to formally apologize for annoying you so much, but I was just so eager to get some of your insight on the world I'm so confused with.

I'm going to be honest when I say I might not remember you in the future. For me, memories fade rather quickly. One of the reasons why I'm writing this letter is in hopes that I will remember your existence because of it. Have an amazing and happy life-full of wonder, adventure, and creativity. I hope you remember me.

Jessica
Los Angeles, USA

P.S. here's another flower

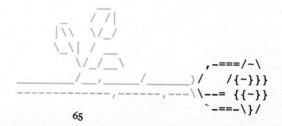

Capital C Colon emoji,

Who knew I would have become friends with
the cute elevator guy. I first saw you in that elevator.
You had no idea who I was, and vice versa. That thing
happened quite a few times, until our first term ended
and I no longer had classes in that building. One
fateful day, I saw you waiting for your queue from
the organization we were applying for. My heart
was literally running for its life. We were assigned
the same room AND the same group.

It was destiny. We introduced ourselves, and after
that event, we became good friends. The next event
commenced, and we hung out half of the afternoon.
You have no idea how much that day means to me.

You have my heart running for its life the way yours
does in those triathlons you talk about.

I just wish it meant the same to you.

Love,

Peach Iced Tea

My Love,

Falling for you was the strangest thing that has
ever happened to me. I can't say I expected it
and I definitely never thought it would happen
the way it did.

Before you, love and everything that came with it
didn't seem all that real to me. In fact I always felt
like something was wrong with me because I had
never had a crush in high school and my first year at
university provided only flings and careless nights.

However something changed when I got to know you,
I suddenly realised what people were talking about.
I liked you more than I thought I could ever like
someone and I wanted to spend every waking moment
with you.

I finally understood why all my friends had wanted to lose their virginities to someone special and I wished I could have gone back in time to experience that with you instead.

The intimacy of sex became clear when I experienced it with you, I felt closer to you than I thought was possible and each time was equally as special as the last.

I also realised the intimacy in the smaller things we shared, a glass of juice in the morning, little forehead kisses, walking your dog or my personal favourite, backrubs as I fell asleep.

My Love, you're my first crush and my first love and as naïve as it may be, I sincerely hope you are my last.

Thank you for everything,

Your Love

Dear **You**,

You're so beautiful. Your smile, your eyes, your lips, your hands, everything. Did you know that you play in my mind like one of my favourite song lyrics, you sting my heart like after eating a bowl of hot soup. You know me but I don't think you see me, I see you for one, I see you like no other, I see you so often your image never leaves the remains of my brain. I wish you see me, I wish you remembered me. I wish that you could see me the way I see you. I see you for you and that is the you that I love, but please can you see me too.

Sincerely

Brianna
Manitoba, Canada

ethereal

poetic

fleeting

volatile

fragile

electric

ambrosial

euphoric

ineffable

efflorescent

distant

transient

foggy

idyllic

haunting

mellifluous

iridescent

blissful

Dear **Ben**,

If only I could write something that sounded like a song. Something that makes your head spin.

How I wish my words could sound like a rhythm that you feel in your heart.

Every letter, like a note that coincides melodiously with the next.

If only I could put the essence of your being into words.

You look like music.
And I can't write anything that would do you justice, but ...

You look like music.

Erika
USA

Dear —— ,

I pushed you away and put up a wall to keep you out.
To keep from getting hurt. I was scared of how I felt.
I was scared I would hurt you, that you would hurt me.
But now I know that you are perfect, perfect for me.
I want you, no I need you. I want to spend every night
holding your hand and be wrapped in your embrace.
I want someone to care about me and protect me from
all that is bad in this world. I just want you. I want you
to love me again like I love you.

Danielle
Australia

Dear **Crush**,

They say after four months, it isn't a crush anymore,
it's love. It didn't take me four months to realise that.

Yours always,

Nathalie
London, UK

Hi **Crush**,

It kind of feels weird writing a letter to someone
whom I've shared memories with.

I still remember the first night we exchanged our
'I love yous' and the first time you held my hand
and told me I'm beautiful.

I have always been the quiet and shy one, while you
always have been the expressive and funny one.
We complement each other, we bring out the best
in each other, and we definitely spread the love to
everyone who comes our way.

You were always there for me, but things took
a wrong turn causing us to drift apart. I was insecure,
and I completely forgot all about you. I made you
leave...

No, scratch that, I wanted you to leave and you did.
It was hard for you, but you know I wanted to find
myself. I went away for college, and I completely left
you hanging.

The funny thing is even though I have pushed you away too many times, you're still there. You told me you'll still be there.

I admire your bravery. I admire everything about you, and all you have ever done for me. I love you, and I'll never forget you. **You taught me how unconditional love really works**, and I'm sure the next person that you'll love will be blessed to have you for life.

Loise
Philippines

Dear ——,

I didn't like the fact you farted on me,
but I still like you very much.

Jada
USA

Dear **Angel**,

All humans search for love,

And now I can stop searching,

For after all,

I am only human.

Anonymous

This Moderr
PO Box 3
Boulder, CO

♡

Love
19
0307 .

('}{")

middle

Gabriela

middle

Relationships. They're everywhere.

But in books, film and television they're often portrayed as this unattainable and unrealistic fantasy. Couples are either fighting with each other or gazing endlessly into each other's eyes. Of course, things are never that black and white. We tend to glaze over the fundamental elements of relationships; the ones which don't involve broken plates and sex in the rain but rather the inner mechanics that make it all work. Relationships in the real world usually aren't as dramatic as they are on our screens, and it's the small everyday things that amount to a much bigger picture. A cup of tea can go a long way, and a simple 'How was your day?' can change a mood instantly. It's those quiet gestures we often overlook that help maintain a stable and happy relationship. →

wanderlust

reverie

cosmic

rainbow

fireworks

kinetic

scintillating

alluring

irresistible

intoxicating

wonderlishious

As a guy who currently has a girlfriend of eighteen months, I'm a big fan of relationships (though of course I would say that). They teach us to be better. We have to be more selfless and giving. We have to think as a team rather than an individual. It's a constant backwards and forwards to understand each other; to grasp how the other person thinks, to recognise how their very being works. Maintaining a successful relationship is a great accomplishment; two people are able to work in harmony and that is something to be proud of.

For this middle part of the book I asked people to submit a thank you letter to their partner. I wanted people to write something to celebrate their relationship. We rarely take the time to just sit and appreciate things. We move at such a fast pace that we neglect to see just how good we have it. I also asked people about how technology affects their relationships. The response we received was lovely and very touching. Clearly the internet is polarising; for some people it works, for others it most definitely doesn't.

It seems quite clear from all the letters that love is still ever blossoming; people are still madly and unconditionally in love despite the rise of social media, and even after many years together. If you're in a relationship, I encourage all of you when reading this to think about your partner. What are you most thankful for? And do you say it enough?

90

Dear **Orestis**,

Thank you for telling me about your newest favorite
songs. I fall in love with every song you tell me about.
And thanks for remembering my favorite constellation
and telling me that when you see it at night you think
of me. It makes me feel really close to you even though
we're half a world apart.

I love you.

Hedda
Norway

Dear **L**,

Thank you.

For the most incredible year of my life.
For showing me the world
For that time you drove 27 hours so I could see my
        best friend
For letting me play Kygo every day
For caring about this beautiful planet that we get to
        call home
For inspiring me to make my craziest dreams a reality
For being the best big spoon
For not compromising your morals
For being such a great salsa partner
For that spark in your eyes and the grin on your face
        when you jump in a waterfall, climb a tree
        or hold a puppy
For wanting to make the world better, and realising
        that that is the most important thing we can do
For helping me find my spark back
For not settling for a mediocre life
        and for not letting me do the same

For preferring to sleep in a van than a 5 star hotel
For helping me live the adventure
For appreciating the magic of every sunset
For choosing me over Beyoncé
For making me feel safe, in every way
For opening your heart to me. I know it wasn't easy,
        but I promise to treasure it.
After all, the biggest adventure you can have
        is to open your heart.

With love,

R

P.S. I'd choose you over Beyoncé too

Technology creates disconnection
in communication.

Phoebe, England

Dear **Cameron**

With your fingers all cut up from the strings on your guitar, and your hair falling over your face like it does every morning. I lay and watch as you sit in pure happiness playing the music you love so much. Noticing all the beauty you have when you look at me and smile, and the small little smile lines that form around eyes that I love so much appear. You are a beautiful human.

Thank you for loving me the way you do and thank you for showing me what love really is and can be. I'm so extremely lucky to love you.

Yours always

Ashleigh
Australia

We would study on skype. 9 and a half hours of just silence. I was never alone though. If one of us travelled to a place where wifi wasn't available as often, we would just film a bunch of videos.

Emilia, Lima, Peru

open

captivating

unwavering

dedicated

consuming

benevolent

giving

flourishing

elevating

patient

liberating

irreplaceable

altruistic

daunting

unconditional

developing

genuine

transformative

Hi **Sam**,

I just want to say thank you for loving me unconditionally – through the best times and the worst times. Thank you for looking at me when I'm broken and my eyes are all puffy from crying and still calling me beautiful. You make me feel like a million pounds.

I love you. To the moon and back.

Anonymous

Dearest **Jack**,

I just wanted to thank you for always buying me food. The combination of your rosy cheeks and a blueberry muffin are my life essentials.

Love,

Julie

Dear **David**,

Thanks for the countless rides home. Also, thanks
for letting tons of half empty water bottles stay on
the passenger side of your car. I know you hate them.
But they're kind of our little collection.

I'm going to be sad when you drive away to college,
and I'm stuck here.

And I'm going to be sad when you throw my water
bottles away.

Audrey
Georgia, USA

I think technology has had a positive effect on love. I'm in a long-distance relationship so it makes separation a lot easier due to Skype, etc. Keeps us in touch.

Finlay, UK

Dear **D**.

Thank you for finding me new books and movies to watch/read every week. I don't think you understand how much I actually appreciate that.

Thanks for not punching me in the face every time I beat your a$$ at Mario Cart. Because I always win.

Also, thank you for letting me listen to Drake real loud in the car... my ex hated me for that.

I like that I like u and I like that u like me

Let's keep it that way.

Thank you.

S.

Dear **Mike**,

I appreciate so many things about you and what you do for me. A short list of these things is: you being the honest, confident, loyal, dedicated man that you are when it comes to your family, your work, your friends, the cashier at the store, at the drive thru, and of course to me and our children. Thank you for feeding me, especially when I am a beast (you know my love for food). For always seeing me as beautiful even when I know I look ragged.

And in this too short of a list I just mentioned to my brother today that I love how you always see both sides to a story and are a very fair person. A character like that speaks volumes and I am so happy to be a part of your life. I love you.

Love, your wifey,

Jess
Michigan, USA
(married for 15 years)

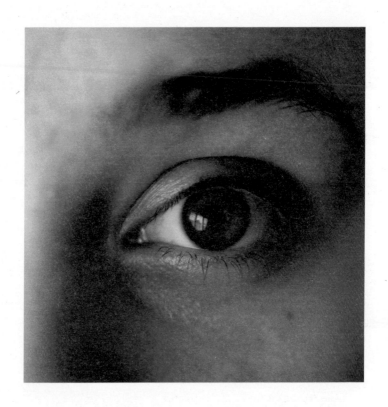

Dear **J**,

I love the passion in your eyes when you do something you love. I can see the excitement radiating through your skin. It's inspiring. You push me to pursue my aspirations.

Thank you for lifting me up when I'm down.

With love,

E

Dear **Joseph**,

Thank you.

Thank you for making me see the stars
when I only saw the darkness.

Agnes
Sweden

Hi **Valentina**,

I'm writing to you because the feelings that I have for you make me do this kind of stuff.

For the last couple of years you and I have been very good friends. You've been my support when I had no one. I can't thank you enough for everything you have done for me. The friendship you've offered me, your love, your tenderness, your kindness, and infinite and unconditional support. My soul and heart will ever be grateful for you, there's no one that makes me feel like you do every day since September 18th.

Soon we will be having our third month anniversary and I know it sounds silly but I've liked and had a crush on you since the beginning of the year so it's a big deal for me. I hope this letter for you will make it to be actually in the book so I will buy the book and give it to you.

With great love to you my beautiful girlfriend,

Alvaro

We got married on facebook before we even started dating... 4 years later and I think we may actually do it someday.

Melissa, Toronto, Canada

Dear **Alex**,

> Alone in cold sheets,
> I imagine us folded like paper
> In our origami bed.
> And it keeps me warm.
>
> Thank you for being there,
> even when you're not.

Love,

Freddie
UK

whirlwind

inconstant

flux

entropy

pandemonium

bewildering

helter-skelter

fickle

brittle

fluctuating

Dieter,

You asked me to marry you and I said yes.

I said yes to adventure.
I said yes to doing your laundry.
I said yes to waking up next to you.
I said yes to driving, when you just wanted to enjoy
the view.
I said yes to baking you bread from scratch in
accordance with your diet.

Thank you for taking me on this trip around the world.
Thank you for standing up for me, when I refused to
stand up for myself.
Thank you for making breakfast on Sundays.
Thank you for wanting me to stay.

Thank you for asking...

Love always,

Simela
New York City, USA

Internet connection in Scotland is fine, but in Mozambique it's shit. Now I notice when the screen freezes he's still cute.

Marila, from Portugal, living in Scotland

Dear **Emmalisa**,

You are currently fast asleep next to me and the butterfly tattoo on the back of your neck is peeking up from the duvet you're wrapped in.

Your short, silver-gray hair is a bit messy from all the sleep, your breathing is heavy and your skin is so soft.

Lying here knowing you are next to me is the most valuable thing for me.

I never thought that long distance relationship would work out, I thought it would hurt too much being away from each other. But it doesn't, because when I walk off that train and see your smile it's like I never left in the first place.

And I'm so thankful for that, I'm so thankful for the little things. Your smile, the way you kiss my forehead, freezing on the balcony together taking the last blow from our cigarettes, when you say you love me, the way your tiny body is filled with beautiful artwork, just being with you.

I just want to say thank you for being the most amazing girlfriend I could ever ask for. and thank you for giving up so much just to be with me, I can never thank you enough.

Now I'm gonna stop writing this thank you note and wrap my arms around you until you wake up.

I love you.

Yours truly

Fanny
Sweden

> texting the love of your life and him reading it 6 days later, thanks for the heads up read receipts

Mareeda, California, USA

Dear **Dan**,

It's a Monday and you're currently having an interview for a job you don't want. There are a lot of things that you don't want to do, but do anyway, you're funny like that. In fact, you spend most of your time doing things for other people instead of yourself.

I wanted to thank you for the things you do for me the most though.

I want to thank you for the undying patience you have towards me, no matter how testing I become.

Thank you for accepting my flaws. Thank you for being strong in a gentle way. Thank you for being my number one fan.

I'm unsure of the future – where it will take us, but I'm thankful for the time I have with you right now – thankful for the 'grow together' type of love we have.

Most importantly, I'm so thankful we are alive at the same time, and being able to hold your hand (they're always really warm – thanks for that too, I guess).

Love from
Little One
(Leah)
Manchester, UK

Dear **Jaemin**,

Recently, I've been writing so many letters to you. You're currently doing your 21-month service in the South Korean army and I miss you so very much.

However, this letter is different from the past letters that I have written to you; this is a thank-you letter. Firstly, I want to thank you for everything you have given me and done for me throughout our relationship. You have given me more love than I could have ever asked for and you have done so many sweet things for me. You are the man that I have always dreamed of meeting and sometimes it still shocks me that we're together. You are so kind, thoughtful, respectful, smart, and so much more. (Dude, I freakin' love you! lol)

Many people ask me if waiting for you is difficult and is it worth it? Of course it's difficult, from seeing you every single day to possibly seeing you twice a year is a very sad thought. Also, are you worth waiting for? To me, waiting for you is the most "worth-it" thing in my life. When times are tough and I miss you like crazy, I just think about my love for you, what it's going to be like when you return, and I am reminded that this is only temporary. Those are the things that get me through the day.

$\rightarrow$

→ I know that I always tell you that I love you, I miss you, and I'm waiting for you. However, I don't think I ever really thanked you. Well, here it is! "thank you!" Why am I thankful? Besides everything that I mentioned before, I am so thankful to you for giving me something that's worth waiting for.

From this experience, I am able to learn what it really means to be patient, what it means to be strong, and what it means to be independent. You have given me a chance to really learn some valuable life lessons and for that I am truly thankful. I want to show you that I am strong and that I can endure through tough situations. I want to make you proud, in the same way that I am so proud of you. Our relationship is strong and special enough that I know that we will make it through these tough months.

Please remain strong and healthy,

I'll see you soon.

Jackie

Dear **Michael**,

We've been together little over a year – that's pretty crazy, isn't it? When I came out, part of the reason I was so hesitant was a fear that I'd never find someone I'd genuinely love. I didn't relate to the gay community in many respects. I was fully prepared to go it alone.

Then, we met. I can't explain the mixture of joy, love and lust that I felt. Combined with an eternal fear that one day you'll figure out that you're better than me and leave me. But I won't let that happen, not without a fight. We've pulled through some pretty major hurdles this year, and we deserve to take the time to be proud of that.

You ground me more than anyone else ever has. Whilst I'm out shooting movies, you're on the streets saving lives as a paramedic. We couldn't be from more different backgrounds either, which in turn means we have so much more to learn from each other.

I'll always love you, and even if we don't stay together, I hope I remain as thankful as I am now for all that you've done.

Harry
x

Dear **H**,

Thank you for always wanting to have sex.

Catarina
Portugal

Dear **Danny**,

You are the definition of cliché;
Showing up at my doorstep with flowers,
Writing poems and love letters,
Framing our memories on your bedroom walls,
And filling up my life with laughter.

So predictable but I wouldn't have it any other way.

To many more years together,

Faly
Singapore

> I personally hate how technology has made me
> unable to communicate my emotions verbally,
> I would kill to undo that.

Gemma

Dear **Goose** (Elliott),

I've got quite a lot to thank you for. Five years is a long time, and over these years I've realised what a huge, gigantic, massive part of my life you have become. To simply put it, you're my best friend, my travel partner, my soulmate (as cheesy as this all sounds), and I really don't know what I'd do without you.

I want to thank you for all the times you've been there for me, through the most difficult part of my life when my father was going through chemo, to the small difficulties like trying to decide whether I should buy those pair of shoes on ebay. I want to thank you for being the biggest support in my life when my anxiety and panic attacks were the worst they had been and how you drove me to every appointment. You were there with me every step of the way.

I want to thank you for all the afternoons together, trekking around shops and going on long walks (even though you don't enjoy them all that much). I want to thank you for making me laugh and smile through every part of the five years, you have always made the biggest effort when it comes to making me happy and I hope I do the same for you.

I want to thank you for deciding to make the decision
to come and meet me all those years ago at the station.
although you only travelled for 2 and a half hours on a train,
it felt like hundreds of miles away. If you hadn't of decided
to travel all that way, who knows where we would be now.

Most of all, I want to thank you for loving me, including my
crazy Christmas-loving side.

From

Goose
(Eve)

It's funny how technology was the reason
my relationship started, but was also the
reason why it ended.

Jovana, Serbia

Dear **Y**,

I love your smile. I love your beard. I love your laugh.
I love how clumsy we are. I love how you are as needy
as me. I love your hugs. I love texting with you in the
middle of the night. I love how we both make wishes at
midnight. I love how ticklish you are.

I love how it has been six months by your side
and I still get butterflies in my stomach.

I love that you were my first love.

I Love We.

Thank you.

Isabele
Brazil

Dear **Y**,

this is my favourite picture of us because what we were feeling in that exact moment was so real that I can't even explain it properly.

I love you.

Isabele
Brazil

Dear ——,

Long distance is never easy but it just makes the time you have together that much more special.

Canada—Wales: we'll be together one day.

Ciara
Canada

Tech is the key that holds us together. But at the same time the key that breaks us. The loneliness goes away.

Ilyas, Florida, USA

Dear **Carlos**,

You were 19 when I took this photograph. I was your first love and first heart break, but your endurance makes you the bravest person I know. You have taught me about self-love and I will be forever grateful.

We are currently tackling with a temporary long distant relationship and now I know what it's like to fully love and be loved in return.

Five years together but still looking forward to more.

I chose this picture because that was an unforgettable beach day. The beer was cold, the weather crisp and all was good. This sums up my life shade with you.

Andrea
Tampa, Florida, USA

Dear **Rasmus**,

I'm glad you can fart in front of me, I am sorry for
pressuring us to take the second cat and I have no
regrets leaving my home country to be with you. I love
you with all my heart and please don't shave.

Alise
Estonia (originally Latvia)

Sometimes I have to restrain
myself from texting him so
we have enough to talk about.

Dora, Czech Republic

Dear **boyfriend**

I want to thank you for loving me, but more
importantly for loving yourself. For you are the most
beautiful human and you deserve more love than
I could ever give.

Thank you for teaching me that the anxiety which
burdens me, does not make me a burden.

Thank you for holding my hand and dancing with me
without occasion.

And thank you for being my first love and for hoping
I'll be your last.

I know you told me that I could share your name.
But even though I am sharing this, no one will ever
feel the way we did. This love belongs to us and your
name tastes better in my mouth than it will ever look
on this paper.

I promise to love you until it is the end.

Your girlfriend,

IHN
Denmark

> How has technology
> changed my relationship?
> It hasn't – I'm still alone.

Brogan, England

Dear **T**,

You're my moon, my stars, you're my sunrises
and sunsets. You're the crisp mountain air, the first
layer of snow, and that steady rainfall after a humid
day. You're just everything. Thank you for being
everything.

Yours,

S

Dear **Jonathan**,

Thank you for confessing your feelings for me in the university's library.

You and I were in an aisle amongst the presence of books and the sound of flustered silence. My face was as red as an apple and as hot as an open flame, yet with my back turned I listened to you utter words that, I reluctantly admit, I really cannot remember. (All I do remember was that you were so incredibly cheesy with your confession that you made my smile stretch from cheek to cheek!)

But more importantly, that feeling of pure bliss and exhilaration I felt back then is one that I still feel up to this day when I'm in your presence.

That was forever ago. Since then, everything slowly changed between us. What I never expected to happen has come to be and still is happening, and I cannot wait (although I am terrified) for what the future brings us.

However...

No matter what happens, the 9th of May will always be a date for me to look back on as a God-given chance at happiness, and I'm more than grateful that it is with you.

Your words and sweet (sometimes ridiculous (in a great way!)) gestures have never failed to make my heart jump-start with endearment. I hope you know that.

Thank you for everything thus far.

Love,

Your Maasimcheeks

Joleene
Guam, Micronesia, USA

Technology has affected my relationships in that I talk more frequently online & it makes me believe my online self is superior to my physical character

Lauren, London

halcyon

digital

anachronistic

yikes

transatlantic

asshole

friendzone

oops

404NotFound

kismet

Richard,

I want to say thank you.

I believe that in relationships, the most important factor is honesty. It is about being with someone you can be honest and show your true self to. That is what love is about. Loving someone at their weakest and vulnerable moments, and supporting them through their proudest moments.

What makes me happy is the little things that you do. always thinking about the smaller things, like having dinner ready for me after a 13 hour shift, not only with a cup of tea, but a bottle of wine in the fridge too. Cosy nights in and watching all the rubbish reality TV with me and never complaining, but completely understanding when I moan about you playing FIFA. Thank you for pausing your rubbish PlayStation games to let me have a girly breakdown about what I should wear for my girly night out.

Nothing puts a bigger smile on my face than just in that one look that you do, you truly make me feel like I am the only girl in the world. There is no better feeling than being in love.

$\rightarrow$

→ Thank you for telling me you love me every morning when I wake up and every night before I go to sleep (without fail!). Thank you for always being there. Always.

Nothing can compare to the true feelings you show me every single day, but what truly puts a smile on my face is that you always put me first (as I will always do for you), and the fact that you are never afraid to show your feelings either. I have never been someone that wears their heart on their sleeve or express their feelings of love, so thank you for teaching me how to love with my whole heart and not just a fragment.

Finally, thank you for understanding and accepting every part of me and allowing me to do the same for you.

x

Anonymous

It was easier to type lies than to tell the truth.

Sam, New Zealand

134

Dear **Dany**,

Thank you
For believing in me
For making me believe in myself
For loving me entirely
Flaws and all

For seeing beyond my imperfections
Beyond the mood swings
All the silly little things
For seeing me, truly

For making me laugh
For also laughing along with me
For being my best friend
And for putting your trust in me

I love you deeply and entirely
With all I have in me

Keren
Venezuela

Dear **Rae**,

Thank you for giving me the kind of love they sing
about in power ballads. I still get teeny butterflies
each time we kiss, even after all this time.

Also thank you for always giving me the sour sweeties
after you found out they were my favourite.

All my love,

Catherine
England

A tangled web of phone calls and text messages gives
us the safety net we need to be further apart.

Sophie, Dublin, Ireland   136

Dear ——,

We've just had an argument. You're sitting at the opposite end of the room. Neither of us has said anything for a full thirty minutes.

It was an argument about something utterly pointless. You thought I did something; I thought you said something else. It was just a miscommunication really. Either way, I'm still sat here frustrated and irritable. We drive each other mad sometimes, don't we?

I wanted to write this letter to tell you that despite my occasional bitterness (like today) I love and care about you deeply. We are and have always been soul mates. And although sometimes we fight, it's these moments that really make me reflect and understand my love for you. It's a testament to our relationship that even at the worst of times there is still so much affection and willingness to make it work, whether we want to say so or not.

Thank you for putting up with me and for not letting my cynicism take over. You are my rock and you mean the world to me.

In an attempt to resolve whatever this was, I'm going to run downstairs and make you some tea. I know camomile is your favourite (hope it is, anyway). Also, sorry for being a dick earlier. I'm all over the place today.

Anonymous
UK

This Modern

Kemp House

152 City Roc

London

EC1V 2NX

Remember to post early for Christmas!
royalmail.com/greetings

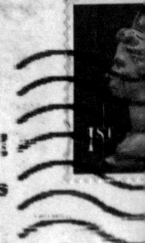

Love

</3

end

Too cloudy to even
understand my feelings.

Elisha
Wales

end

Well, here we are. The end.

The morbid reality of relationships is that they really only have two outcomes. It either works out or it doesn't. Not everyone you meet will be 'the one'. It can take many years, and many people to find someone you want to settle down with.

This necessity of finding your soulmate is a fairly new idea. If we jump back fifty years, it was very common to marry someone who could provide stability rather than affection. We would tend to marry out of safety rather than passion and the very idea of a soulmate was quite uncommon. Nowadays, *all* we're looking for is our other half. We're looking for that person who fundamentally gets us; the person we were destined to meet.

And all of that pressure we put on ourselves to find that person often ends in one way. Heartbreak. We want the people we meet to fit a very specific image in our heads and in doing so we neglect to see what they are truly like. And when we eventually do, we're left so disappointed that we often want to start from square one again.

$\rightarrow$

aching

heartbroken

self-destructive

desperation

extinguished

delusion

melancholic

shattering

unworthy

infuriating

adrift

hurtful

asunder

excruciating

incomprehensible

perfidious

dumped

over

Let's be real here. Breakups are the worst. Of all the things we have to deal with, coping with heartbreak is right up there. We feel so many conflicting emotions and we're stuck in what appears to be an endless limbo. It's a never-ending state of not knowing how to feel, and only with real time are we able to make sense of things.

I remember feeling fundamentally lost during my breakup. I'd wake up every day and not know what to do with myself. My own independence scared me and I didn't feel comfortable doing things on my own. I suppose you make a team with your partner when you're in a relationship, and it took me a while to adjust to being alone.

In retrospect, the loneliness was probably the hardest thing. You feel like nobody understands you and as a result you can alienate yourself from everyone. You're basically just super-erratic. I think that's the point I'm trying to make here. You're completely irrational and it's difficult to come out of yourself and recognise that.

The idea of the whole book really stemmed from this stage of relationships. Initially it was going to be a book for the broken-hearted, and I'm so happy that it's turned into something more all-encompassing, and hopefully more upbeat. And although the book ends on a rather sombre note, it's important to see the positives in the letters. For whatever reason it may be that things didn't work out, it is the lessons learnt that will live on and will help guide us all to the next person, and maybe the right person. Somebody who will help mend and reinforce, rather than break and weaken.

dear **jake**,

you ruined so many songs for me.

Katherine
New Mexico, USA

Dear **Cal**,

I have a bookmarks folder of articles I would have sent to you if we were still talking.

Moll
UK

Dear **Pedro**,

Remember the day of this photo? My friend took it without us knowing. That day I cooked a chocolate cake for us. It was the very beginning of our story. It has been a while since that day, and since we were a couple.

We're not talking to each other so often anymore, but I wanted to say how much this photo means to me. It was the day that I first said 'I Love You' to you. It was the first time I said these words for someone in the strongest way of its meaning. For my first boyfriend.

Although we've had some bad times in our relationship during and after its end, the good memories will stay on my mind regardless of the bad ones.

Because they say the first time we'll never forget. And it's true.

I forgive you.

Vinicius
Brazil

Dear **A**,

I am 99% sure you have my childhood Pokemon card collection. When we parted ways you placed my possessions in a bag and left the bag outside my house. The Pokemon cards weren't included.

Sorry I drunkenly messaged you asking if you had stolen my Pokemon cards. Sorry that was the first thing I said to you after saying nothing for three years. Thanks for a great time, I mean it.

I hope you are OK.

As always,

Soph
UK

Dear **Boy**

You once told me that in the space of two years every cell in your body regenerates.

There will come a day when I can reclaim my own skin, when my flesh will have never been touched by you.

Never yours,

Girl
New Zealand

Dear **Jamie**,

I'm not sure at what point during our short but sweet relationship you decided to cheat on me, and I'm not entirely sure that you know just quite how much it has affected me.

Without your secrets and lies I wouldn't have to second guess every little detail of every relationship that followed. Without you, my current boyfriend would not have to spend hours of his time reminding me that I can trust him or that I'm good enough for him or that he's not like you. Without you I would not be filled with doubt and worry and anxiety every second of my life.

But I guess all of this is okay because you got hurt exactly the same way 12 months later.

What goes around comes around.

From

Charlotte
UK

Dear **Zack**,

You stole my tongue and took my tastebuds with you but I still taste the color red on my lips.

I tasted the color blue when it was over and black when we didn't try again.

Pink when your words faded from my memory and green when I saw your words on another girl's lips with red in her cheeks.

I never noticed your gray eyes.

Most sincerely,

Annie
USA

Dear **TX**,

I do consider you to be an ex.

I do think of you as the first woman.

And I did love you (in a way).

You were never a fling, but the pièce de résistance to my entire sexual and emotional renaissance.

I'm sorry I led you to believe otherwise.

SH
USA

Dear **Joseph**,

This is a poem I wrote for you, my love.

<u>Stars</u>

How I long to
feel
your presence   next to mine,
to dream of your
fingertips caressing
my worries and
turning them into
glittering stars
in the night
enhanced only by the
pale glow
that your eyes,
like the moon,
radiate in the
cool, dark night.

Annette
USA

Dear **Ben**,

Would you kindly keep your topless snapchat selfies to yourself. No they do not make me want you. And no I do not understand 'dem bedtime feels'.

Also a word of advice if you ever hope to attract a girl; try less pout and more personality.

Peace (no love),

Shanahbelle
Australia

Dear **Agustin**,

It's been five continuous years of me holding his hand, and still feeling like I'm reaching for yours.

Lorena
Argentina

Dear **Boy**,

I loved you like a brainless zombie, ever searching for your warmth, and yet now I cannot see what it was that drew me to you.

Only remnants of old lost love are still lingering in my heart, and yet I am curious as a child to know what you're doing tonight.

I guess I am like a battle-hardened spider sitting on an old love-spun web, always ready for an attack, but still getting disoriented every time you fly by.

Come to me, little B, let me tell you a story...
my love may sting, but don't you worry.

Edita
Lithuania

Dear **Oliver**,

You were sent away on Monday. I watched your girlfriend burst into tears when she heard; it was in English class. I sit right behind her.

She reeks of perfume, and if her peroxide drenched hair doesn't make my eyes bleed, the neon tank tops do. On the big day, however, her eyes were bleeding mascara while mine tried to hold back the tears of joy.

You called me the night before you left, reminding me that you still loved me. Am I the only person you told? I still don't understand why it was a surprise Monday morning when the teacher broke the news.

Why do you torture me with your love? Unlike your girlfriend, I can't show emotion. I can't let everyone know that you "get the girls" and that I am a "slut". I was always the second thought.

I'm so happy you're gone, because it's my time to understand myself and stop living in this terrible, hushed limbo you have me stuck in.

You were my first love, and I was your hidden lust. Oliver I fucking hate you. I hate everything about you. I hate your hazel eyes, chapped lips, conditioned hair, strong neck, the shape of your nose, and the sound of your laugh.

I am moving on. I am excited for the future. I can do this. I will find peace. Starting tomorrow, I'm sitting in the front of class; I'll be sure to wear all black.

Love,

Ashley
USA

puzzling

unpredictable

enigmatic

imponderable

tantalising

improbable

ambivalent

misleading

unexpected

strange

Dear **You**,

<u>Six years</u>

Yes, I still count them
I couldn't make us last, I'm sorry
Could've been an epic love story
Letting go was all for me
Selfish and naive, I broke your heart
Years have passed
I wish I loved you more
Every day I'm haunted by the absence of you
The what-ifs and could've-beens
Songs of loss, on repeat
23rd of January was our mark
My heart breaks, as I embark
A new love that will complete me
Self love, this is what's meant to be

Mareeda
United States

Dear **Josh**,

Time.

I cried through the weeks and thought the heartache caused was beyond repair.

Time was the healer. Time is always the healer.

Unexpectedly, I found myself smiling and looking up to the sky realizing I'm okay.

Hanna
Iceland

Dear **Jacob**,

Sadness always licked at the feet of our love but we still never chose to wear shoes.

I found myself a pair of boots now, I hope you've found some too.

Hannah
UK

Dear **Victor**,

Was it easy for you?

Because it killed me.

Anonymous
USA

Dear —— ,

You told me it was no strings attached but somehow
I became tangled.

Still in love with you

Anonymous

168

Dear **Darren**

Sorry I was a bit of a bitch, can we be friends?

Lauren
UK

Dear **Joe**,

I lied, you never made me orgasm.

Megan
England

Dear **Rodri**,

I truly hope you find someone who makes your heart sing in the same way my own did every time you kissed my flaws.

Gràcies per estimar-me.

Ariadna
Menorca, Spain

Dear **T**,

Today I saw you in the park,
you were holding her hand and kissing her cheek.

Meanwhile I was hiding behind the trees,
whispering to the wind:
'Be happy and follow your dreams'.

Rowan E.
Spain

Dear **Daniel**,

Years past and your song still echoes around me.

Pain drums into the night, your words of love now
redundant in waves and vibrations, repetitive
melodies, tired harmonies of what was and could've
been and that breakbeat rhythm you left my heart in.

But why can't I stop listening?

Kyra
UK

Dear **James**,

I don't agree with the way you went about it, adultery should not be the way out but I understand that you may have felt it was time to go. We spent 7 happy years together with our eyes covered in a veil of daily routine.

Since we are now apart, I can see that it wasn't meant to be. We were so young when we became partners and in that time we grew into ourselves. I still stand by what I said when we broke up 'I am me because of you' but now we are apart I am still me and I stand here on my own two feet, proud of who I am and how I handled this situation.

I have since learnt that I needed more from a companion. Someone who would ask how my day went, someone who wanted to spend time with me. We thought it was important to be our own people but I think we lost sight on the importance of love, the importance of spending time in each other's company and being in a relationship together, not alone.

I'm still working on forgiveness for what you did to me but I have an unearthly understanding of why you may have ended things. The universe spoke and opened our eyes to the world. I am now awake and I'm ready with open arms for someone who will love me, explicitly, with all their heart.

Lauren
England

Dear **Jason**

I forgive you...

I forgive you for always putting yourself ahead of
my needs and saying those hateful words in the end.
I understand now we both needed to grow up and
mature. I survived.

While I don't know where you are or what you are
doing I like it that way. You were mean, abusive and
you destroyed every bit of self-esteem I had. To this
day I work on my issues with my spouse.

You messed me up so bad. I felt like I didn't deserve to
live on this earth and I was stupid and naïve. I wanted
to end it but I had people in my life who took me out
of the toxic relationship we shared. The fact you called
my mother and fed her so much lies. Getting her to
call me and yell at me for being mean to you. You left
me with nothing in a city where I knew few people.
You drained our bank accounts and left me to figure
things out on my own.

I pawned my engagement ring and went home to my parents. I will never forget my Mother's face when she came to get me in the airport. She cried so much when she saw me. The daughter she raised and loved wasn't there. My parents had to listen to me scream in my sleep. Had to help me through the panic attacks when friends and family would come around. I had to push myself to get better.

But I forgive you. I forgive you because I survived and if I can get out of a relationship that was that toxic I have hope that other women can too. I have hope as I found the love of my life. Even though it was rough in the beginning he and I sailed through the storm and are conquering my demons. Most of which were caused by you.

I survived and I am becoming a stronger person. I have someone who wants to help take care of me, who wants to spend time with me, who loves me for me. I fell in love with the most amazing man. I Survived.

Cassandra
Canada

dear **ex**,

sometimes love isn't skyscraper building,
all defeating,
all-encompassing.
sometimes that's okay.

im sorry i couldn't offer you what you need
what you deserve.

i miss your hugs,
your face when i make you laugh,
your cold toes under the covers,
the heights i had to reach to kiss you,
the long nights over the screens of our phones,
the stuffy study sessions,
your you

your support, your friendship, your love
meant everything to me and
i will cherish it
but im sorry it isn't returned

if only i could love you the way you loved me

maybe then we could have loved more

love,

Rachel
England

P.S. say hi to your mum for me, i miss her cooking

Dear **Max**,

She said I would meet you one day.
Your name would start with an M.
You would change my life.

There we were.

Here I am.

There you are,
still holding my heart.

Madison
USA

Dear **Alberto**,

You've got fat. It's been four years since I put on 4kg
and you told me I was fat. Now you are. And even
though I truly hope you are happy, I am still going to
smile every time a picture of you appears on Facebook.
Because Karma exists.

Keep enjoying food as much as I do.

Adela
Galicia, Spain

infatuation

frightening

deceitful

irksome

arduous

obdurate

half-stalking

someday

strength

Dear ——,

I never knew how good life could be until you came into my life. I never knew how happy someone else could make me feel.

You made me want to get up every morning. I had something to look forward to when I got off work. I couldn't wait to get to your place to open the door and give you a hug and a kiss.

So when you broke up with me I didn't know what to do. I went from having you in my life every day to nothing. I went to bed alone and I woke up alone. It felt like you were giving up on me, giving up on us and everything we had been through. It hurts when the person you love says you aren't their best chance. It still hurts.

I thought I was your best chance and I'm convinced I can be that guy for you. But you made your mind up, and it hurt you so bad even thinking of hurting me that you couldn't eat, you couldn't sleep. I keep playing back moments in my head, thinking what did I do wrong?

$\rightarrow$

→ But maybe I didn't do anything wrong; I just didn't do enough right. And I realize that now. I should have been more open with you; completely transparent. How can you be with someone who doesn't want to open up? That's not a healthy relationship, and I understand that now. I was so scared to lose you that I became a shell of myself.

All I wanted to do was make you happy. Seeing you smile or making you laugh brought me the greatest joy. I tried to go the extra mile to make you happy. I think the saddest people always try their hardest to make people happy because they know what it's like to feel absolutely worthless and they don't want anyone else to feel like that. I didn't feel worthless with you, I felt like I could take on the world when you were by my side.

I should have expressed this sooner, opened up more, and let my guard down. I should have done more for you, for me, for us. I spent the last eight years of my life running away from my feelings. I'm tired of running. When you broke up with me all I wanted to do was talk to you. I wanted to hold you; I wanted to cry to you.

I miss you. I miss holding your hand; I miss the face
you make when I try my horrible English accent. Most
days when we were together I would wake up and
look at you, and think that this was the person I would
wake up next to for the rest of my life.

I still find pieces of you in my life. Whenever an
Ed Sheeran song comes on I think about that night
we slow danced to *Thinking Out Loud* in the hotel room
after Coachella. Whenever Chris wears the tie you
got him I think about Oxnard and how great a day it
was. Whenever I get in an Uber I think about how you
would always slide to the middle seat just to hold my
hand.

Whenever I wake up I think about you, whenever I go
to sleep I think about you.

You'll always be in my soul, my mind and my heart.

My love always,

J

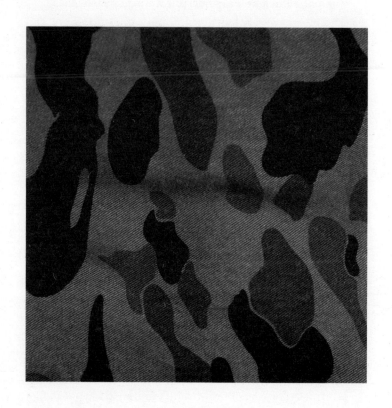

Dear **Emmanuel**,

Watching you talk was my favorite. The passion
and the drive I heard in your voice were present in
every conversation we had. It's why I could never
stop falling in love with you. You were damaged and
artistic. You were intelligent and intriguing. You were
not afraid to challenge me on my bullshit. You weren't
the ideal boyfriend. Not at all what every girl wants.
But you were everything I could ever want.

Watching you grow personally is an experience that
I will always be thankful for. Your drive and your
optimistic pessimism inspired me and grounded me
at the same time. Something only you and I could
understand. There were a lot of things about each
other only you and I could understand, things that
won't ever be understood by anyone else. I am who I
am today because of whom you are. I don't need ten
years to go by to know that you will be the one who got
away. I can't do anything about it: right person, wrong
time. I will forever be thankful for you, Emmanuel,
but God does it hurt to lose you.

I miss you. Like a lot more than I would like to admit.
I feel like at this point, days after we finally decided to
end things for good, I'm still a little numb to the pain.
It comes in 30-second waves. Little things will happen
that'll make me remember you and will make my eyes
tear up, but I'll be fine a few seconds later. I've never
felt like this. I don't know if it's good or bad. I don't
know if the pain is

$\rightarrow$

$\rightarrow$ going to gradually come back and then hit me all at once. I feel like I'd do anything to get you back. But at the same time, I know that at this moment we can't be happy with each other because you just don't have the ability to try right now.

I miss you so much though and I really wish it weren't that way. You were my everything, you were who I pictured spending the rest of my life with, raising kids with, all of it. It's so weird to think it won't be like that again. It's weird to think I won't wake up to you or go to sleep next to you every night of my life in the future. It makes me so sad, I cannot bear the thought of anyone taking your place in the visions I had for us.

Before you I never gave a fuck about anyone else's happiness. After you, your happiness was all that mattered to me, even if it meant compromising my own. I'm so in love with you that the only thing that brings me true happiness is seeing you happy.

I remember when you had that bad experience with your dad, and you cried to me. It took everything in me not to break down. It hurt me so much to see you hurt. I had never felt that much pain from seeing someone else hurt. That was the first time I told you I loved you. Because I knew I did. That was a week after we started dating, four months after we started talking again. As fast as that may have been, I had no doubt, I still have no doubt that I did and do love you so much.

All we need for us to work is to try. I tried so hard without success because you made no effort whatsoever. I want so badly for you to tell me you miss me and that you want to try this again, because I think it could work. That probably won't ever be the case again though.

Even when you're a total asshole, I'd choose you over anyone else on the planet. I don't know how I feel about you being so indifferent. I'm happy you're not in the amount of pain I'm in, but I'm sad I'm in so much pain over someone that could not care less about me.

Ivette
USA

Dear **Wince**,

Thank you for giving me the best remembrance that I'll treasure for a lifetime, our son, Ryze.

Love,

Karen
Philippines

Dear **Father-of-my-Child**,

I wish that I had never told you I was pregnant. I wish that I had broken up with you as soon as I found out, and carried on with my life having you never find out that my child was also yours. I wish that it was possible for me to have this wonderful human being without you.

I wish I had never given our relationship a shot, I don't think the pain was worth it. I sometimes wish that you would wake up one morning and decide that you just don't want to be a dad anymore.

But mostly, I wish that you would just see how much pain you have caused and how much heartbreak you continue to put both myself and our child through.

Catherine
Canada

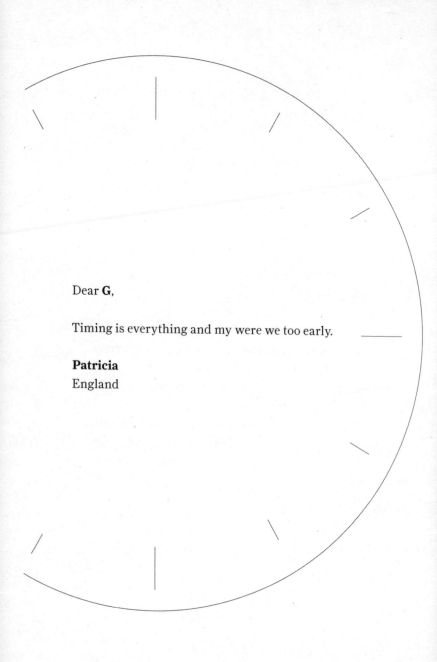

Dear **G**,

Timing is everything and my were we too early.

Patricia
England

Dear **Collin**,

Thank you for being the guy to help me realize
I'm utterly and completely a lesbian.

Rachel
New York, USA

Dear **breakfast waffles and that fairground ride, tickle fights and twitches**...

The first to hurt my heart.

With 40 minutes between us, also a job or school, you became my Saturday and my Sunday.

I loved you, pure and simple, would have done anything to have kept it up and am sorry that wasn't enough.

A weekend of heartbreak and lonesome thoughts, you say we're just friends now.

"Go away", "just leave" my heart a darkened mess, "I love you" "I miss you" you tease me a glimpse of hope.

To crash again with these feelings in my head but you're gone, you're gone again.

→

OOOOOOO| →

→ I tried your password just to see, not expecting it to work but nothing to hide you said?

She messaged you a Wednesday and asked you to come round, you messaged me that same night, just happened to say something else?

Monday night I called, shaking and distraught, you so calm it made it worse, "what did you do that Wednesday?" a numbing tone did answer, chased by a text, a simple "go away".

Curled up in my covers, all contact cut and that heartbreak haze.

A strange numb feeling... I feel I miss you yet goodbye.

With memories,

Anonymous

Dear **you**,

I would love if you would give me my heart back, so I can actually mean the word "love" when I use it again.

Yours even though I know better,

Habiba
Egypt

almost

I think almost is a pretty good and epic word to define us.
We were almost there, we almost made it.
Like Frank Sinatra once said, the pieces almost fit.
You almost loved me the way that I loved you.

Patricia
Portugal

Dear **Ethan**,

You made me little. You shrunk me down. Slowly at first, then all at once. Your comments and critiques turned you into a sculptor, scraping away at me piece by piece. With careful precision you crafted me exactly to your liking.

The vitriol in your remarks became apparent, and your words in passing became demands. With each day my body would parade how little you really had made me. You left me with no self worth, you left me with no sense of who I was without you, and then you just left. You left me feeling as though I would never be enough. As though I had become too little for you.

But then, I realized all along, that it was you who was little. You made me feel little to make yourself feel big. You kept me in my little box because you were afraid of how big I could become all on my own.

In the end, the best day of my life was the day I realized that I could grow without you. I made big plans, that didn't include you. I dreamt big dreams, that didn't include you. It was from your seeds planted in bitterness that I grew. You made me big. Thank You.

Meaghan
Toronto, Canada

Dear **David**,

Please, be a better friend to her than she was to me.

Anonymous

Dear **guy who I used to know,**

I wish you never took me to the movies in my favorite cinema. I wish you never took me to my favorite restaurant. I wish you never spent christmas with me. I wish you never took me to Amsterdam. I wish you never kissed and hugged me in my room. I wish you never told me that you loved me at my favorite spot in my hometown. I wish you never gave me my favorite book for my birthday.

You're gone now, but all my favorite places and things still remind me of you. They aren't my favorite places and things anymore.

Anonymous

I've never been in love,
and that terrifies me.

Trisha
USA

[and Trisha wrote again, later:]

I do want to let you know that my story about love has
changed.

I am 26 now and think I am in love, it still terrifies me!

Wish me luck!

All the best,
Trisha
USA

Dear **Lost Lover**,

The sound of your voice has slowly d r i f t e d from my memory

Lately I have found it hard to remember your favorite color

Or the shirt of yours I once loved

I've realized that I am slowly forgetting everything about you

Similar to a sandcastle too close to the water

Slowly washing away with time and eventually completely vanished

As if it was never there

Slowly traces of you have faded away and soon you'll be just another broken dream

A dream that I held too close to my heart for far too long

Kayley
USA

Dear **T**,

When I came to stay in your family home last summer you said something to me that held so ironic, so beautiful and poignant, so unfair. You hushed each syllable as gently as you'd hushed my lips close after rubbing cocaine in my gums. You said to me: I never really feel like I'm living, you know? Like not a lot of life goes on when I'm at home. But I feel like what we're doing now is what I'd always dreamed living would be like.

You had no idea that a month prior to me being wrapped in your duvet I'd tried to kill myself and a month later I'd be pregnant with your child. That living to me had become tiresome and the potential of life we'd made together and make together, those four days that I still talk about as though they still mean something, were the most alive minutes for the two of us even if only for a moment. They made me effervescent.

You arsehole and you brute, you boy and you human heart. You gave me purpose. A purpose that could grow to call me mother and a purpose that could teach me how to love the world I was existing in. You gave me splendour and you gave me haikus, you gifted me a fluttering in my veins that I hoped to be eternal.

$\rightarrow$

→ When you stole those things from me, when you proposed to split an abortion like a dinner bill, when you stopped calling at 4 am to read me Leonard Cohen, when you decided some other girl's hand was more worthy to hold I thought you'd taken everything.

Now I dive from sleep to awake in a hurtled flailing most nights, thoughts that tumble through pirouettes and languid movements, they all bend and curve around my flat stomach that could still be round. They fill its emptiness with a heavy confetti of a thousand tiny expectations of what this baby could've looked like. What they might have achieved. What we could have brought up in a broken unison.

What I fear you misconstrued, when I told you I was pregnant after you'd got back with your ex-girlfriend, is that it meant I was pregnant with a future of us. A future where you still kissed me outside of your dad's office or where you touched my breasts under my shirt at the back of the bus. I wasn't pregnant with those broken nostalgias, I was pregnant with the hope of a new life. The notion that the unborn could spur me reborn and that rebirth would stop me wanting to curl up into the foetal position and drown.

I thought you'd ripped my inner most feeling right from the gut of my passion, you denied me the right of motherhood and you denied me the right to hold your love. You denied me.

What I didn't realise you had done, what I am still working so hard to imagine when I wake every morning – is that even though my rolled cigarettes don't taste like the tips of your fingers from honeyed toast, I am fine. I am strong. I am wise.

And thank god; in a broken hallelujah, I am not yours. I'd never meant to be. I am mine and mine to learn to love as wholesome as I realised I could for the living and unborn.

In a bizarre conclusive curtain call, I'm only writing to say – thanks for teaching me the B side of Etta James is better, that egg whites should be whipped before folded, that my body is worth worshipping. That 'exquisitely exquisite' is a phrase to be versed more often. You dissolved a lot of goodness from within me but you built me tools unknowingly that would make me see beauty again.

C
UK

TALLAHASSEE FL 323

27 NOV 2015 PM 3 T

This Mod

PO Box 3

Boulder, C

rn Love.

9

0 80307

[O⁻]

gallery

love in 10 shots

by
Christina, **Deborah**, **Jessica**, **Katy** and **Loeka**

Close

Closer

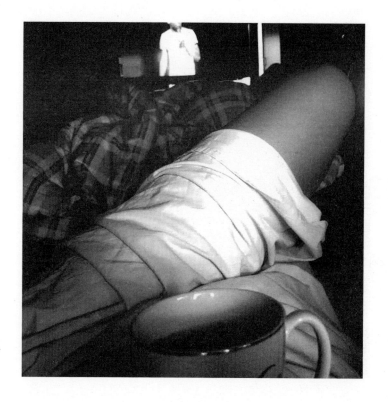

Comfort

Uber

Surprising

Dangerous

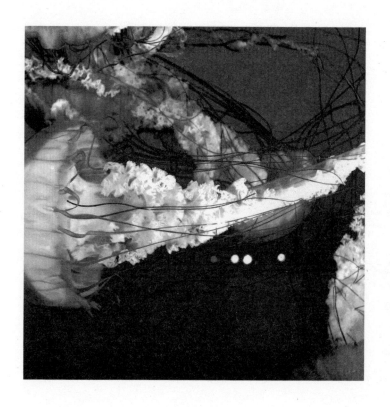

Stings

Hold on

Infinite

Love yourself

Dear —— ,

I see love as dedication, just like writing a book.

Last summer, I had surgery on my left (dominant)
hand, which was not initially supposed to render my
hand unusable, but there were complications – aren't
there always? It has taken me an entire year to regain
the range of motion and strength in my wrist/hand,
and I had to re-learn how to write and play my violin.
It was a stupidly long and painful recovery, but here I
am today writing pages and pages of words that mean
so much to me.

I have shared a photo of a page from one of my
journals that I used during my recovery (hence the
wacky handwriting). The photo is a reminder that I
wrote to myself, 'I love you,' because sometimes you
just need to say that to yourself until it feels true.

This experience taught me to love and appreciate
the imperfections life throws at you, and roll with
the punches.

Love your lumps, bumps, battle scars, birthmarks
and the things that make you you! Perfection is
overrated anyways.

Katy

thanks

This Modern Love was a dream of mine; it's a dream come true thanks to everyone who submitted. Words cannot describe how grateful I am to all of you who wrote a letter, sent a picture or tweeted.

Thanks to my mum, my brother and especially my dad for all your help and encouragement. I wouldn't have been able to do this without you; you eased a lot of the pressure from my shoulders.

Thanks to my girlfriend Arden, for your unwavering support as always. To Giles Cowan and Nick Hayward at The Narrative, for overseeing the project and for providing the emotional backup. Thank you Laura Chernikoff, for keeping everything organised, and for being there to aid any creative ideas. Thanks to my lawyer Brian Carr for all his wonderful work.

A huge shout-out to Tim Barnes for designing the book and for putting up with my meticulous emails. Thanks to my publishers at Penguin Random House and Simon & Schuster for all their hard work. The biggest thanks to Ben Brusey, my editor, for giving me this opportunity and for keeping me afloat. Your ideas and support are this book; thanks for putting up with me for a year.

Finally, a massive thank you to my friends and my viewers for sticking with me. Your constant positive reinforcement keeps me going. I love you all terribly and I hope you like the book as much as I liked putting it together.

Will